C000137348

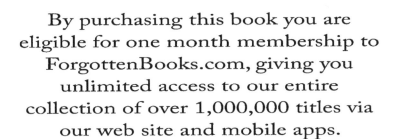

ISBN 978-0-260-02362-9
PIBN 10922927

Texas Christian University

Its Equipment

Texas Christian University has a plant valued at $598,200.00, with every modern convenience, situated in an ideal college community, combining all the advantages of a city life with all of the excellencies of the good, old country. It has forty-three years of splendid history behind it. Into this institution have gone the blood, tears and sacrifices of some of Texas' most devoted citizens. It has a faculty of seventy-nine members, selected for efficiency and for complete sympathy with the institution's high educational purposes. It has a campus of fifty acres, upon which is erected five buildings of twentieth century fire-proof construction and artistic design. It is situated in one of the most progressive cities in Texas. Fort Worth has thirteen railroads radiating in seventeen directions, which make it accessible from every part of the Southwest. It is a city of beautiful homes, paved streets and high educational and social ideals.

Its Standards

Texas Christian University is a standard A grade college for men and women, so classified by the United States Bureau of Education and the State Association of Colleges of Texas. Special departments in piano, voice, violin, expression, domestic science, painting, commercial branches, medicine and education. The University specializes upon its standard courses leading to degrees, but offers a number of special courses for which diplomas and certificates are awarded.

Its Aims

Texas Christian University has, as its aim, Christian character, Christian scholarship, Christian idealism. Its supreme aim is to furnish our splendid commonwealth with young men and women who will serve and who are possessed of the qualities of real leadership. Texas Christian University prides itself upon the health of its students, the home atmosphere, the beauty of surroundings, its clean athletics, its true and noble manhood and womanhood and the spirit of gentility in all things.

TEXAS CHRISTIAN UNIVERSITY BULLETIN

VOL. XIV.   JANUARY, 1918   No. 1

Texas Christian University

SUMMER SCHOOL

Fort Worth, Texas

JUNE 10 TO JULY 19
1918

PUBLISHED QUARTELY BY

TEXAS CHRISTIAN UNIVERSITY

ENTERED AS SECOND CLASS MAIL MATTER AT THE POSTOFFICE AT FORT WORTH, TEXAS

TEXAS CHRISTIAN UNIVERSITY.

SUMMER SCHOOL

OFFICERS OF ADMINISTRATION

Executive Committee of Trustees

S. J. McFARLAND....................................Chairman
H. M. DURRETT..........................Chairman pro tem.
JAMES HARRISON, R. M. ROWLAND, H. W. STARK,
V. Z. JARVIS, DR. BACON SAUNDERS.

Executive Committee of Faculty

EDWARD McSHANE WAITS........................President
CLINTON LOCKHART . ...Dean
CHARLES I. ALEXANDER...........................Secretary
E. R. COCKRELL, W. M. WINTON, CHAS. H. ROBERTS.

OFFICERS OF SUPERVISION

WALTER E. BRYSON.....................Dean of Deportment
MISS TYLER WILKINSON....................Dean of Women

H. M. DURRETT..............................Business Manager
MISS LILLIAN DURRETT . ...Registrar

SUMMER SCHOOL FACULTY

EDWARD McSHANE WAITS,
President of the University.

CLINTON LOCKHART, Ph. D., LL. D.,
Dean of the College of Arts and Sciences.

E. R. COCKRELL, A. M., LL. M.,
Principal of Law School.

C. I. ALEXANDER, A. M.,
Professor of Mathematics.

W. M. WINTON, M. S.,
Professor of Biology.

E. C. WILSON, Ph. D.,
Professor of Education.

JOHN R. McCLUNG, A. .M.,
Professor of Chemistry.

WALTER E. BRYSON, A. M.,
Professor of English.

CHAS. H. ROBERTS, A. M.,
Principal of Academy.

MRS. LENA GARDNER,
Instructor in Academy Mathematics.

MISS MERLE HOLSAPPLE,
Instructor in Academy Languages.

MRS. E. R. COCKRELL, A. B.,
Principal of Department of Painting and Drawing.

MISS LEILA LONG POWELL,
Principal of Department of Oratory.

J. A. DACUS,
Principal of College of Business.

MISS LALLA BRIGHT CANNON,
Teacher of Voice.

CARL RUPP DOERING,
Teacher of Piano.

MISS ALINE WEIR WILSON,
Teacher of Piano.

MISS ANNA McLENDON,
Teacher of Sight Singing and Piano.

SAMUEL P. ZIEGLER,
Teacher of Public School Music.

MISS VESTA BURFORD, A. B.,
Principal of Domestic Science.

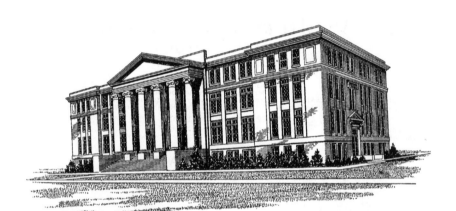

THE ADMINISTRATION BUILDING OF TEXAS CHRISTIAN UNIVERSITY
This building is one of a group of five noble structures that adorn the campus of Texas Christian University.

SUMMER SCHOOL

PURPOSE OF THE SUMMER SCHOOL

The courses of the Summer School are offered mainly for four classes of students:

1. College Students, who wish to bring up some delinquent branch, or to remove some condition on previous studies, or to lighten and shorten the remainder of their work for a degree.

2. Preparatory Students, who desire additional credits toward college entrance, or to lighten the task of the Freshman year, or to secure advanced standing.

3. Teachers, who take advantage of summer studies to improve their scholarship, or to promote their college advancement between terms of teaching.

4. Special Students, who wish to advance their attainments in Music, Oratory, Painting, Business, the Bible, Home Economics, and other branches, although such work may not lead to a particular degree or standing in college.

VALUE OF THE SUMMER SCHOOL

The value of summer work in college is ever becoming more apparent. The theory of a long summer vacation is now antiquated. This is an active age, and whether he wills it or not, every man is in competition with every other man, and no man has time to throw away. Much of means and thrift are being lost in war, and students like others must help to retrieve. The call of the world to them is urgent, and the period of education is too brief and precious to waste.

Summer studies, being free from many distractions incident to other terms, yield better training and better grades than others.

The expenses are fewer and lighter in summer than in any other season.

Not only is a long summer vacation a delusion, but college in summer escapes a temptation to waste time or fritter it away in some luckless enterprise.

In cool buildings and spacious classrooms, pleasant and effective work is independent of summer heat.

Summer credits stored up on the University records are a precious asset for future prosperity.

To musicians, artists, and prospective business people, the Summer School is an agency of advancement that may not be neglected.

ADMINISTRATION BUILDING, LOOKING SOUTH

6

To prospective soldiers, it is very important to learn French and German before going abroad.

Those who may teach in private schools, or who already hold State certificates, yet desire to specialize in some particular field of teaching or private study, or to do certain advanced academic work, should find a good opportunity in the Summer School.

LOCATION

Texas Christian University is situated in the extreme Southwestern portion of the city of Fort Worth, directly accessible by street cars. A broad, open country stretches to the South and West with nothing to obstruct the summer breezes. It has five magnificent new buildings, well equipped and modern in every respect. It is high, overlooking the city, with beautiful scenery in all directions. It is an excellent place for a pleasant and profitable summer's work.

FORT WORTH AN ATTRACTIVE CITY

Fort Worth is modern in every respect, and is probably the most progressive city in the State, most typical of the foremost ideas of Southern people. Its school buildings and college buildings have the most approved forms of educational architecture and equipment. It is a great railroad and commercial center, active and enterprising, and affords its visitors an interesting study and profitable observation. Its fine artesian and lake water supply and pure, fresh air render it the most healthful and enjoyable place for summer work.

ADMINISTRATION BUILDING

The Administration Building is a massive four-story structure, built of re-inforced concrete throughout, faced with cream-colored brick, and is absolutely fireproof. Floors, ceilings, staircases—all parts of the building except doors, windows and facings for them—are absolutely incombustible.

The equipment of all science rooms is thoroughly up-to-date, and the student has no lack of opportunity for securing adequate information through experimental methods. The chapel is one of the finest in the South. Its dimensions are ninety by fifty feet. The platform is thirty-six by thirty feet in size, and is well equipped with dressing rooms on the wings. Its seating capacity, counting gallery space, is over one thousand.

It is safe to say that no more suitable and complete equipment for class room or lecture work is to be found in any institution in the land. The rooms, all of ample size, lighted, and are provided with the most approved furniture.

NORTH END OF ADMINISTRATION BUILDING, LOOKING TOWARD JARVIS HALL

This building contains the Department of Fine Arts, including Music, Painting and Oratory; the Business College; and the halls for the literary societies. The Music Department is equipped with new Knabe pianos, and has splendid practice and instruction rooms. The Business College is allotted ample space and is also well furnished. The literary societies have beautiful halls. The liberality of students and friends has rapidly given these halls the equipment to which they are entitled. In the Administration Building the University has a workshop worthy of her ideals and unexcelled in facilities for producing that culture which is the object of the school.

GOODE HALL

Goode Hall, so named because of the liberality of Mrs. M. A. Goode, of Bartlett, Texas, who was one of the principal donors to the building fund, is a substantial structure 130x140 feet, built of re-inforced concrete and brick throughout, and therefore, like the other buildings on the campus, absolutely fireproof. This building will be open to teachers with their families.

JARVIS HALL

The dormitory for young ladies is beautiful in form and finish, and is an exquisite product of the builder's art. Severely in harmony with the general plan adopted for the group of University buildings, its classic grace and dignity are not only restful to the eye, but are also an inspiration to noble thought and life. Like the Administration Building, it is constructed of re-inforced concrete throughout, and is therefore fireproof.

CLARK HALL

The third dormitory completed is almost a duplicate of Jarvis Hall. It is a splendid dormitory for men and is fitted with electric lights, parlors, free phones, and all modern conveniences.

BOARD AND ROOM

Board and room may be had at the University at $6.75 per week. Irregular meals, 35 cents each. The University reserves the right to alter these rates with changing war conditions. The Clark Hall, as described above, will be open to men, and the Jarvis Hall to women. These buildings are new and modern in style and furnishings.

Those desiring to have special rooms reserved should send a deposit of $2.50 to Business Manager H. M. Durrett. This deposit will be credited on room rent.

All students will be expected to furnish their own bed covers, bed linen, and toilet articles. A set of bed linen should be brought in suitcase, since a delay of other baggage may be embarrassing.

THE ADMINISTRATION BUILDING

This is a massive, four-story structure, built of re-enforced concrete throughout, faced with cream-colored brick. The equipment is thoroughly up-to-date. It contains the Depart_ment of Fine Arts; laboratories, class-rooms, and the administrative offices. The building cost $175,000.

DIRECTIONS

On arriving at the University, all students should go to the Business Office in the Main Building, where they will be directed to rooms or to the proper committees for classification and assignment of studies.

REGULATIONS

Conditions of entrance into any College or Department are the same as those announced in the University Catalogue. Likewise, the same system of credits, the same number of recitation periods, and the same plan of examinations and grades apply as in other terms. Students, however, are not permitted to take more than nine credits in the six weeks, whether the work be review or new study.

FEES

No matriculation fees in any department.

Tuition fee, College or Academy, full course........$16.00
Tuition fee, College or Academy, ⅔ course......... 12.00
Tuition fee, College or Academy, ⅓ course......... 6.40

Laboratory fees in Chemistry $10.00 for the summer, in Biology $6.00.

Rates of tuition in the College of Business, Music, Domestic Science, and Painting, will be found in connection with the statement of the work on pages following.

All fees are due at the time of enrollment, and will be collected at the main office of the University.

VALUE OF SUMMER CREDITS

In order that the summer work may be equal to that of any other term and the credits of the same value, the teachers are required by a set schedule to give as many hours of recitation to a branch of study in the summer term as in other terms. Accordingly, credits received for summer work will count at full value for any college degrees or State teachers' certificates. Official time schedules of recitations will be bulletined in the main building some time before the summer term opens.

11

JARVIS HALL

This residential hall is beautiful in form and finish, an exquisite product of the builder's art, its classic grace and dignity are not only restful to the eye but are also an inspiration to noble thought and life.

COURSE OF INSTRUCTION

The following courses are to be offered in the Summer School. The University may substitute another branch if the number of pupils should be insufficient to justify the work in any study.

BIOLOGY
Prefossor Winton.

11. General Biology, nine (or six) credits. Class work and laboratory. Nine credits for freshmen and sophomores, six credits for juniors and seniors. Prerequisite to any other course in this department.

CHEMISTRY
Professor McClung.

1. General Inorganic Chemistry, nine credits to freshmen and sophomores, seven credits to juniors and seniors. Lectures, recitations, and laboratory work.

24. Organic Chemistry, nine credits. Lectures, recitations, and laboratory work.

EDUCATION
Professor Wilson.

A first grade State certificate, valid for four years, to teach in any public school in Texas is obtainable by the five college credits, including nine credits in Education. Accordingly the summer course in this department covers its work for the State certificate.

11. Educational Psychology, three credits. The aim is to apply psychological theory to educational practice Special emphasis will be placed upon recent experimental work in the psychology of instruction. An introductory course.

13. School Efficiency (Management), three credits. A study of the problems of organization and control of class and school.

15. Methods of Teaching, three credits. A study of the factors that govern elementary school subjects, the methods of learning, or securing attention, and of meeting student individuality.

24. Modern Elementary Education, three credits. A study of modern ideas as applied to elementary schools.

29. Educational Hygiene, three credits. A survey of hygienic conditions and needs in public schools of every grade.

32. Play and Playgrounds, three credits. The psychol-

CENTRAL HIGH SCHOOL BUILDING.

Modern in every respect, representing a total outlay of
$294,409.52. Fort Worth has one University, two A class col_
leges, nine private and preparatory schools, four business col_
leges, twenty-six public schools, with 14,000 scholars, cost of
buildings being $1,613,211.20.

14

ogy of recreation and the conditions that best contribute to the true interest of play.

Three of the above courses, in all nine credits, selected by the demand, will be offered.

ENGLISH

Professor Bryson.

11. **Rhetoric and English Composition, six credits.** A comprehensive study of the principles of rhetoric and a thorough practice in writing English; analysis and criticism. Required of all freshmen.

38. **Elizabethan Drama, six credits.** A first-hand study of the drama between Udall and Shirley, with special emphasis upon Shakespeare.

ENGLISH BIBLE

Professor Lockhart..

31. **Messianic Prophecy, six credits.** A survey of the work of Old Testament prophets and its bearing upon their Messianic announcements. An exegetical study of all the passages that are usually regarded as Messianic.

33. **Monuments and the Bible, three credits.** A study of Babylonian, Assyrian, Egyptian, and Palestinian inscriptions recently discovered, with their bearings on the contents of the Bible.

HISTORY

Professors Lockhart and Cockrell.

24. U. S. History, the Colonies, three credits.

25. U. S. History, 1789 to 1865, three credits.

26. U. S. History, since 1865, three credits.

31. Revolutionary Period in Europe, three credits.

MATHEMATICS

Professor Alexander.

12. **Plane Trigonometry, three credits.** Preparation for this course includes Algebra (at least through quadratic equations) and Plane and Solid Geometry.

13. **College Algebra, three credits.** A review of quadratic equatoins with complex numbers, permutations and combinations, probability, theory of equations, determinants, and fractions.

21. **Plane Analytical Geometry, six credits.** The relation of the equation to the locus; and translation of geometric conditions into algebraic terms.

23. **Astronomy, three credits.** Mainly descriptive, intended primarily as a culture course.

Three of the four courses just listed will be offered.

SOCIAL SCIENCES

Professor Cockrell.

17. **Political Science, three credits.** Text: Introduction to Political Science, Gettell.

35. **Modern City Problems, three credits.** Text: Chapters from Beard; lectures; assigned work.

15

A DRIVEWAY IN FOREST PARK.

Fort Worth has many beautiful parks. Forest Park, which contains a 'Zoo," lies within ten minutes' walk of the campus of Texas Christian University. It is a favorite place for the students of the summer school to resort and to have their evening lunches under the wide-spreading trees.

16

THE ACADEMY

The Academy connected with Texas Christian University offers the usual high school courses of study, however, with many better facilities than most high schools possess as respects library and laboratories. The rate of tuition per unit course undertaken will be $16. The following courses are provisionally announced:

LATIN .
Miss Holsapple.

Caesar and Prose Composition, one unit.

MATHEMATICS
Mrs. Gardner.

Second Year Algebra, one unit.

Plane Geometry, one unit.

PHYSICS
(Teacher to be selected.)

Elementary Physics, with laboratory experiments, one unit.

SPANISH
Miss Holsapple.

One unit, at least, in Spanish will be offered, subject to demand.

TARRANT COUNTY COURT HOUSE.
The most magnificent county building in the South. This building is constructed of Texas granite and occupies one of the leading beauty centers in the city.

SUMMER SCHOOL OF MUSIC

PIANO

Professor Doering.

Mr. Carl Rupp Doering graduated at the Sternberg School of Music at Philadelphia and at the Leipzig Royal Conservatory of Music at Leipzig, Germany.

He is a pupil of Constantin von Sternberg and Robert Teichmuller.

The summer course of six weeks will be directed toward the needs and demands of music teachers and will include the subjects of Piano Technic and Aesthetics, Interpretation and Musical Form in their relations to piano playing.

Fees: Two half-hour periods per week: $21 for the term of six weeks. One period per week: $13 for the term.

Mrs. Doering.

Mrs. Doering graduated at the Leipzig Royal Conservatory of Music at Leipzig, Germany, and was an assistant of Robert Teichmuller, director of the Leipzig Conservatory.

Mrs. Doering will offer a course in Modern Piano Technic, based upon the latest developments of the weight and relaxation method of playing.

Fees: Two half-hour periods per week: $18 for the term of six weeks. One period per week: $11 for the term.

STUDIES WITH PROFESSOR ZIEGLER

Professor Samuel P. Ziegler studied Cello under D. Hendrick Ezerman, of Amsterdam, Holland, now head of Philadelphia Conservatory; studied Harmony, Counterpoint, and Fugue under Richard Zickwer, President of Philadelphia Musical Academy, who was a pupil of the great Richter; for two years member of Faculty of Philadelphia Musical Academy.

CELLO

1. Fundamental exercises, scales, etc.
2. Etudes, duets, and easy pieces.
3. Advanced etudes, solos, and concert pieces.

Two lessons a week, twelve lessons, $18.00.

HARMONY

The study of scales, intervals, triads, seventh chords, and their inversions.

19

THE FIRST CHRISTIAN CHURCH.

Fort Worth is a city of beautiful churches. This is one of our outstanding religious temples, erected at a cost of $150,000. Fort Worth has 105 other churches, representing almost every religious faith and ministering to the upbuilding of the city religiously.

Easy modulations, suspensions, and Harmonization of melodies.

Two lessons a week, tuition fee, class $6.00, private $10.00.

COUNTERPOINT

Simple counterpoint in two, three, and four parts.
Same terms as Harmony.

HISTORY OF MUSIC

Beginning of Opera, Oratorio, and Instrumental Music; Composers of Classic and Romantic Schools; Modern Music and Composers.

Terms same as Harmony.

PUBLIC SCHOOL MUSIC
Professor Ziegler.

The design of these courses is to prepare men and women to teach music in the public and high schools.

Teachers and Supervisors of music in public schools must be qualified to teach Harmony, History of Music, Sight Singing, and Musical Appreciation. They will need also a well rounded education and a love for the work. Some knowledge of string and wind instruments used in the orchestra is recommended. Hence the following courses are offered:

1 Ear Training.

Pitch, Rhythm, and Notation which represents them. Chord recognition, simple modulation, and transposition. One hour a week. Tuition $6.00.

2. Sigh Singing. Singing in common keys, beginning with simplest problems in pitch and rhythm; two, three, and four part singing. One hour a week, tuition fee $6.00.

3. Public School Music. Methods and material for teaching in primary and grammar grades.

High School methods. Outlines of teaching Harmony, Musical History, and Musical Appreciation.

Musical Activities, including preparation of programs, etc.

One hour a week, tuition fee $6.00.

PIANO
Miss Aline Wilson.

Miss Wilson was a pupil and the assistant of the late Rafael Joseffy, and her teaching experience has been both extended and successful. Her work has been very valuable in the University during the past two years.

In addition to her work with other pupils, Miss Wilson will give especial attention to those desiring to make a profession of teaching and teachers desiring to do additional work.

Fort Worth boasts of its beautiful homes.

Tuition for the term: Full time, $15.00; half time, $8.00.

STUDIES WITH MISS McLENDON

Miss Anna McLendon is a graduate of Texas Christian University College of Music with three years of post graduate study and a teaching experience of two years.

SIGHT SINGING AND EAR TRAINING

This course includes training for public school work. The lessons are given in class meeting two hours a week. Tuition $5.00.

PIANO

A course of two lessons a week, one-half hour each, for six weeks is offered by Miss McLendon. Tuition $10.00 for the six weeks.

VOICE

Miss Cannon.

Miss Lalla Bright Cannon studied under Sergei Klibansky and assisted him in his studio in New York, formerly leading vocal instructor in Stern Conservatory, Berlin, and previous to this Miss Cannon had other notable instructors in New York; was soloist in a church in New York and sang with the Rubinstein Club.

Voice Culture **and** Singing, two, three, or four lessons per week. Voice placement, consisting of correct breathing, resonance, tone, evenness of scale, intonation, diction, ..exibility, with phrasing and interpretation.

A cross-street in the business section.

SCHOOL OF HOME ECONOMICS

Purpose of the School

The primary object of this school is to develop young women in all womanly ways and graces and prepare them to become worthy makers and preservers of the home. The courses of study are prepared to secure for the student a thorough understanding of home-making.

Such a purpose has two forms: First, to supply a scientific study of foods, clothing, shelter, and the care of the sick, serving the ends of economy, art, health, and convenience. Second, to enable the student scientifically to perform the professional offices of artistic dressmakers, milliners, caterers, dietitians in hospitals, and house decorators.

Equipment

Large rooms in the Administration Building of the University have been well furnished with individual gas stoves and every modern article that may contribute to the latest and most practical methods of cooking. Likewise ample equipment is at hand for sewing, dressmaking, drawing, and decorating. A strictly modern dining room has been fitted out for this Department. The University has regular departments for Chemistry, General Economics, bacteriology, and Painting, all of which are available for students of this school.

DOMESTIC SCIENCE

Cooking and Serving 12, three credits, if Chemistry precede.

1. A study of the production, manufacture, and composition of typical foods, their classification according to the food principles and the study of the relation to the needs of the body.

2. A study of the cookery processes and their application in the cooking of typical foods.

3. A study of the principles involved in the cleaning and caring for the various sorts of utensils and materials found in the kitchen.

Tuition fee, $16.00; food supplies, $6.00.

Meal Serving 22, three credits, if Cooking 12 and Chemistry precede. Special stress on cost and conservation, and work on war substitutes. Laboratory lessons, a continuation of course 12, only in a higher form. Tuition fee, $16.00; food supplies, $8.00.

A Fort Worth Office Building, in which is housed one of our prominent banks.

DOMESTIC ART

Sewing 12, three credits.

This course is arranged for those wishing to begin sewing in the elementary form. Learning the stitches, both plain and decorative, and the making of simple underwear by hand is given special stress. Patterns used will be drafted by the students. Tuition $8.00.

Sewing 22, three credits, if Sewing 12 and Textiles 22 precede. Pre-requisite, Sewing 12 or its equivalent. Blouses and dresses are made with a certain amount allowed for the expenditure of each. Tuition fee $8.00.

Textiles 22.

Pre-requisite, Chemistry 11 or 14. Study of the different fibres, their growth, manufacture, etc. Also the weaving and spinning processes. Testing of wool, cotton, and silk for adulterations and impurities. Lessons on weaving. This course will be given if the demand is sufficient. No tuition fee for those who take sewing.

SUMMER SESSION OF THE ART DEPARTMENT

Mrs. E. R. Cockrell—Instructor.

The Art Department will hold its usual summer session of six weeks. A term's work can be done in this length of time, as a lesson is given every morning, six days in the week, from eight until twelve o'clock.

This summer term of the Art Department has come to be one of the most successful of the whole year. All students remaining for it are seriously intent upon accomplishing as much as possible. There are very few diverting activities at this time of the year, and because of fewer pupils the instructor can give much personal attention to each one.

The art rooms are well situated for summer work, being in the main building, where they are cool and well ventilated, and all surroundings are conducive to good work.

Mrs. Cockrell will have charge of the summer work with what assistance is necessary according to the size of the class. The following branches will be taught:

Charcoal Drawing.

Oil, Water-color, and Pastel Painting.

Tapestry.

China Painting.

Art Supervisor's Course.

Tuition for the entire term of six weeks is $20.00. Less time may be taken at a proportionate division of price.

T. C. U. COLLEGE OF BUSINESS SUMMER SCHOOL

Beginning June 10 and continuing for four weeks, the College of Business will give the following Certificate Courses:

BOOKKEEPING

This course will meet the needs (1) of those who want to prepare for the State Examinations, (2) those who want a brief course in accounts that will enable them to keep an average set of books, (3) those who want to teach a brief course in connection with their regular school work. Tuition fee, $6.00.

BUSINESS PENMANSHIP

This course is offered especially for those who want to teach Arm Movement Writing in the public schools. Methods of teaching it in the various grades will be thoroughly treated. Tuition fee, $8.00.

SHORTHAND AND TYPEWRITING

Credits will be given in these subjects to those who do not complete them. Those who desire to review their shorthand and typewriting will find this an excellent opportunity. Unfinished courses may be completed by correspondence. Tuition fee, $10.00.

For further information address

T. C. U. COLLEGE OF BUSINESS,
Fort Worth, Texas.

SCHOOL OF ORATORY

Miss Leila Long Powell, Principal.

One of the regular yearly teachers in oratory will offer in the Summer Session courses in physical culture, training for the speaking voice, interpretation of the printed page, and dramatics. All pupils will receive private instruction. Work done at this time will receive credit in the School of Oratory.

Miss Julia Duncan has been detailed by Miss Powell for work in the Summer School.

Tuition: Two lessons per week, $15.00.

MEDICAL DEPARTMENT

The Fort Worth School of Medicine, the Medical Department of Texas Christian University, will run in continuous session during the war and as long thereafter as conditions demand. While the course itself is not to be shortened, the elimination of vacations allows the student to graduate slightly over a year earlier than under ordinary conditions. This feature should appeal to mature men, teachers and others who have often contemplated the study of medicine but have hesitated because of the long time required for the course.

The following announcement is made for prospective medical students who are in the draft age: The Surgeon General of the Army intends, as long as conditions permit, to allow medical students to enlist in the Enlisted Medical Reserve Corps; and to leave them on inactive duty until their professional training is completed. Students may not join this Corps until they are actually medical students.

In brief, the following are the entrance requirements for admission to the study of medicine: 14 units from an accredited high school plus two years of college work, including specified courses in Biology, Chemistry, Physics and a modern language.

The session for 1918-1919 opens June 10, 1918, and ends February 10, 1919.

Interested persons should send for the Medical College Catalog which may be obtained, on request, from:

DR. S. A. WOODWARD, Dean,
Fort Worth School of Medicine,
Fort Worth, Texas.

THE COLLEGE BRED MAN IN BUSINESS AND IN POLITICS

DR. CHARLES THWING made a study of fifteen thousand one hundred forty-two eminent men mentioned in Appleton's Encyclopedia of American Biography to find the facts especially with regard to the relation between college training and success in political life and in amassing wealth. Of the one hundred wealthiest men in the United States he found that in proportion to the total number in America possessing a college education there were 277 times as many college-bred men who had amassed great wealth as there were of noncollege-bred men. In proportion to their numbers in the population, the college men have become Members of the National House of Representatives 352 times as often as the noncollege-bred men; Members of the Senate 530 times as often; President 1,392 times as often; Justices of the Supreme Court 2,027 times as often. Of the more than 10,000 prominent and successful men in all lines mentioned who were still living, 58 per cent were college graduates and 75 per cent had had some college training. On the whole, the college-bred man had attained enough eminence to be mentioned in such a cyclopedia 870 times as often in proportion to his number as the noncollege-bred man.

IN THE WAR that shall follow after the war the school, the laboratory, and the workshop are to be the battlefields. The weapons which science places in the hands of those who engage in great rivalries of commerce leave those who are without them as badly off as were the dervishes of Ondurman against the maxims of Lord Kitchener.

THE EDUCATED MIND is the greatest producing agency in the world, without which fertile soil, timbered land, and mineral deposits are so much useless material. The state or the church that fails to educate dooms its children to industrial and intellectual servitude by those from that state or church that educate.

THE UNITED STATES GOVERNMENT has spent the first six months of preparation for the European War in conscripting brains. We need thousands of other young men and women to take the place of those who are going to the front. What are you doing to prepare yourself for service? Texas Christian University offers unusual facilities for training young men and women for national and for world service.

31

THE NEED OF TRAINED MEN WOMEN TO MEET THE EXIGENCY OF THE HOUR

1% OF COLLEGE GRADUATES HAS FURNISHED:

55% of our Presidents,

36% of the Members in Congress,

47% of the Speakers of the House,

54% of the Vice-Presidents,

62% of the Secretaries of State,

50% of the Secretaries of Treasury,

67% of the Attorneys General,

69% of the Justices of the Supreme Court.

50% OF THE MEN COMPOSING THE CONSTI-TUTIONAL CONVENTION WERE COLLEGE-BRED.

INDUSTRIALLY AND COMMERCIALLY education pays. The United States Bureau of Education also shows that every day spent in school pays the child $9.00. Here is the proof:

Uneducated laborers earn on the average $500 per year for forty years, a total of $20,000.

High school graduates earn on the average $1000 per year for forty years, a total of $40,000.

This education required twelve years of school of 180 days each, a total of 2160 days in school.

If 2160 days at school add $20,000 to the income for life, then each day at school adds $9.02.

THE BOY OR GIRL THAT STAYS OUT OF SCHOOL TO EARN LESS THAN $9.00 A DAY IS LOSING MONEY, NOT MAKING MONEY.

Texas Christian University affords the opoprtunity for an all round training, for statesmanship, and for citizenship, for business and for the professions.

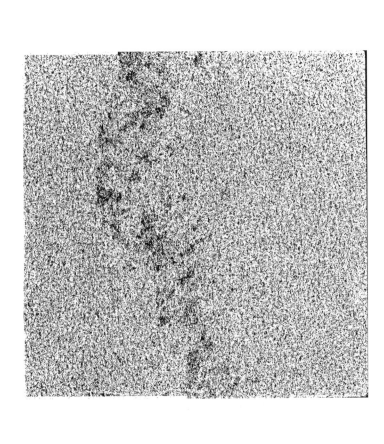

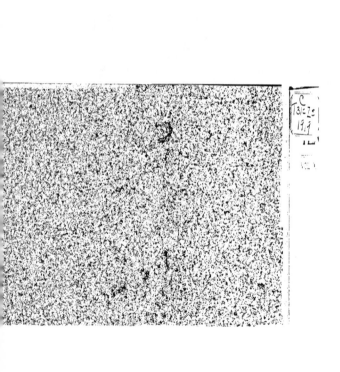

TEXAS CHRI UNIVERSITY BULLETIN

VOL. XIV.   DECEMBER, 1918   No. 4

versity

1919 SUMMER SCHOOL

Fort Worth, Texas

JUNE 9 TO JULY 18
1919

LISHED QUARTERLY BY

TEXAS CHRISTIAN UNIVERSITY

ENTERED AS SECOND CLASS MATTER AT THE POSTOFFICE AT FORT WORTH, TEXAS

VOL XI

T

ENTERED

TEXAS CHRISTIAN UNIVERSITY BULLETIN

VOL. XIV.   DECEMBER, 1918   No. 4

Texas Christian University

1919 SUMMER SCHOOL

Fort Worth, Texas

JUNE 9 TO JULY 18
1919

PUBLISHED QUARTERLY BY

TEXAS CHRISTIAN UNIVERSITY

TEXAS CHRISTIAN UNIVERSITY
SUMMER SCHOOL
OFFICERS OF ADMINSTRATION

Executive Committee of Trustees

S. J. McFARLAND...Chairman
H. M. DURRETT............................Chairman pro tem.
JAMES HARRISON, R. M. ROWLAND, H. W. STARK,
V. Z. JARVIS, DR. BACON SAUNDERS.

Executive Committee of Faculty

EDWARD McSHANE WAITS........................President
CLINTON LOCKHART...................................Dean
CHARLES I. ALEXANDER..........................Secretary
W. M. WINTON, CHAS. H. ROBERTS.

OFFICERS OF SUPERVISION

W. B. HIGGINS........ ....Dean of Deportment
MRS. E. W. McDIARMID.....................Woman Principal

H. M. DURRETT............................Business Manager
MISS LILLIAN DURRETT...........................Registrar

SUMMER SCHOOL FACULTY

EDWARD McSHANE WAITS, A. B.,
President of the University.

CLINTON LOCKHART, Ph. D., LL. D.,
Dean of the College of Arts and Sciences.

E. R. COCKRELL, A. M., LL. M.,
Principal of College of Law.

C. I. ALEXANDER, A. M.,
Professor of Mathematics.

W. M. Winton, M. S.,
Professor of Biology.

E. C. WILSON, Ph. D.,
Professor of Education.

JOHN DAVIS, A. M.,
Professor of Chemistry.

J. R. RICHARDS, A. M.,
Professor of Modern Languages.

E. W. McDIARMID, A. M.
Professor of Philosophy.

WALTER E. BRYSON, A. M.,
Professor of English.

R. E. ROUER, LL. B.,
Attorney and Professor of Law.

P. E. STEARNS, A. B., LL. B.,
Attorney and Professor of Law.

CHAS. H. ROBERTS, A. M.,
Principal of Academy.

O. B. DOUGLASS,
Instructor in Academy Physics.

RILEY AIKEN,
Instructor in Academy Languages.

MRS. E. R. COCKRELL, A. M.,
Principal of Department of Painting and Drawing.

MISS LEILA LONG POWELL,
Principal of Department of Oratory.

MISS CAROLYN CRISP,
Teacher of Oratory.

J. A. DACUS,
Principal of College of Business.

FREDERICK M. CAHOON,
Teacher of Violin.

MRS. HELEN FOUTS CAHOON,
Teacher of Voice.

CARL RUPP DOERING,
Teacher of Piano.

MRS. CARL RUPP DOERING,
Teacher of Piano.

SAMUEL P. ZIEGLER,
Teacher of Cello, Harmony and Public School Music.

MISS GLADYS TURNER,
Principal of Domestic Science.

THE ADMINISTRATION BUILDING

This is a massive, four-story structure, built of re-inforced concrete throughout, faced with cream colored brick. The equipment is thoroughly up-to-date. It contains the Department of Fine Arts; laboratories, class-rooms, and the administration offices. This building cost $175,000.

SUMMER SCHOOL

The great war has closed, and we are now faced with the task of building a new world out of the wreck of the world that was. The character of this new world will be determined by the kind of leadership which comes forward in this hour. The problems of the new world into which we have entered are moral, as well as intellectual, problems; and no man or woman will be able to grapple with them unless disciplined in body, mind and heart. Texas Christian University has weathered the storm of war times and war experiences. She is like "the ship that has found herself" and is launching out upon another era of achievement. The institution recognizes fully the sentiment of Lowell,

> "New occasions teach new duties;
> Time makes ancient good uncouth;
> They must upward still, and onward
> Who would keep abreast of Truth."

PURPOSE OF THE SUMMER SCHOOL

The courses of the Summer School are offered mainly for four classes of students:

1. **College Students,** who wish to bring up some delinquent branch, or to remove some condition on previous studies, or to lighten and shorten the remainder of their work for a degree.

2. **Preparatory Students,** who desire additional credits toward college entrance, or to lighten the task of the Freshman year, or to secure advanced standing.

3. **Teachers,** who take advantage of summer studies to improve their scholarship, or to promote their college advancement between terms of teaching.

4. **Special Students,** who wish to advance their attainments in Music, Oratory, Painting, Business, the Bible, Home Economics, and other branches, although such work may not lead to a particular degree or standing in college.

VALUE OF THE SUMMER SCHOOL

The value of summer work in college is ever becoming more apparent. The theory of a long summer vacation is now antiquated. This is an active age, and whether he wills it or not, every man is in competition with every other man and no man has time to throw away. The call of the world to the student is urgent, and the period of education is too brief and precious to waste.

Summer studies, being free from many distractions incident to other terms, yield better training and better grades than others.

The expenses are fewer and lighter in summer than in any other season.

Not only is a long summer vacation a delusion, but a college student in summer escapes a temptation to waste time or fritter it away in some luckless enterprise.

ADMINISTRATION BUILDING LOOKING NORTH

In cool buildings and spacious classrooms, pleasant and effective work is independent of summer heat.

Summer credits stored up on the University records are a precious asset for future prosperity.

To musicians, artists and prospective business people, the Summer School is an agency of advancement that may not be neglected.

Those who may teach in private schools, or who already hold State certificates, yet desire to specialize in some particular field of teaching or private study, or to do certain advanced academic work, should find a good opportunity in the Summer School.

LOCATION

Texas Christian University is situated in the extreme Southwestern portion of the city of Fort Worth, directly accessible by street cars. A broad, open country stretches to the South and West with nothing to obstruct the summer breezes. It has five magnificent new buildings, well equipped and modern in every respect. It is high, overlooking the city, with beautiful scenery in all directions. It is an excellent place for a pleasant and profitable summer's work.

FORT WORTH AN ATTRACTIVE CITY

Fort Worth is modern in every respect, and is probably the most progressive city in the State, most typical of the foremost ideas of Southern people. Its school buildings and college buildings have the most approved forms of educational architecture and equipment. It is a great railroad and commercial center, active and enterprising, and affords its visitors an interesting study and profitable observation. Its fine artesian and lake water supply and pure, fresh air render it the most healthful and enjoyable place for summer work.

ADMINISTRATION BUILDING.

The Administration Building is a massive four-story structure, built of re-inforced concrete throughout, faced with cream-colored brick, and is absolutely fireproof. Floors, ceilings, staircases—all parts of the building except doors, windows and facings of them—are absolutely incombustible.

The equipment of all science rooms is thoroughly up-to-date, and the student has no lack of opportunity for securing adequate information through experimental methods. The chapel is one of the finest in the South. Its dimensions are ninety by fifty feet. The platform is thirty-six by thirty feet in size, and is well equipped with dressing rooms on the wings. Its seating capacity, counting gallery space, is over one thousand.

It is safe to say that no more suitable and complete equipment for class rooms or lecture work is to be found in any institution in the land. The rooms are all of ample size, lighted, and are provided with the most approved furniture.

JARVIS HALL

This residential hall is beautiful in form and finish, an exquisite product of the builder's art; its classic grace and dignity are not only restful to the eye but are also an inspiration to noble thought and life.

This building contains the Department of Fine Arts, including Music, Painting and Oratory; the Business College; and the halls for the literary societies. The Music Department is equipped with new Knabe pianos, and has splendid practice and instruction rooms. The Business College is allotted ample space and is also well furnished. The literary societies have beautiful halls. The liberality of students and friends has rapidly given these halls the equipment to which they are entitled. In the Administration Building the University has a workshop worthy of her ideals and unexcelled in facilities for producing that culture which is the object of the school.

GOODE HALL

Goode Hall, so named because of the liberality of Mrs. M. A. Goode, of Bartlett, Texas, who was one of the principal donors to the building fund, is a substantial structure 130x140 feet, built of re-inforced concrete and brick throughout, and therefore, like the other buildings on the campus, absolutely fireproof. This building will be open to teachers with their families.

JARVIS HALL

The dormitory for young ladies is beautiful in form and finish, and is an exquisite product of the builder's art. Severely in harmony with the general plan adopted for the group of University buildings, its classic grace and dignity are not only restful to the eye, but are also an inspiration to noble thought and life. Like the Administration Building, it is constructed of re-inforced concrete throughout, and is therefore fireproof.

CLARK HALL

The third dormitory completed is almost a duplicate of Jarvis Hall. It is a splendid dormitory for men and is fitted with electric lights, parlors, free phones, and all modern conveniences.

BOARD AND ROOM

Board and room may be had at the University at $7.25 per week. Irregular meals, 35 cents each. The University reserves the right to alter these rates with changing conditions. The Clark Hall, as described above, will be open to men, and the Jarvis Hall to women. These buildings are new and modern in style and furnishings.

Those desiring to have special rooms reserved should send a deposit of $2.50 to Business Manager H. M. Durrett. This deposit will be credited on room rent.

All students will be expected to furnish their own bed covers, bed linen, and toilet articles. A set of bed linen should be brought in suitcase, since a delay of other baggage may be embarrassing.

DIRECTIONS

On arriving at the University, all students should go to the Business Office in the Main Building, where they will be directed to rooms or to the proper committees for classification and assignment of studies.

CLARK HALL

The home of the young men, has also been recently equipped as a Y. M. C. A. center and, in addition to the other comforts, has a reading room, with the latest magazines, bowling alleys, and pool tables, which are under the supervision of a Y. M. C. A. secretary.

REGULATIONS

Conditions of entrance into any College or Department are the same as those announced in the University Catalogue. Likewise, the same system of credits, the same number of grades apply as in other terms. Students, however, are not permitted to take more than nine credits in the six weeks, whether the work be review or new study.

FEES

No matriculation fees in any department.

Tuition fee, College or Academy, full course... ... ...$16.00
Tuition fee, College or Academy, ⅔ course 12.00
Tuition fee, College or Academy, ⅓ course 6.40
College of Law rates on request.
Piano, two half-hours a week..................... 21.00
Piano, one half-hour a week...................... 13.00
Voice, two lessons a week........................ 22.50
Voice, one lesson a week......................... 13.00
Cello, twelve lessons 18.00
Violin, twelve lessons........................... 18.00
Harmony, two lessons a week, class.............. 6.00
Harmony, two lessons a week, private............. 10.00
Counterpoint, same as Harmony.
History of Music, same as harmony.
Public School Music, 1 hour a week............... 6.00
Painting, etc., work six weeks................... 20.00

Painting, etc., work less time, pro-rata.
Cooking and Serving............................. 22.00
Sewing, either course 8.00
Textiles 3.00
Oratory, two lessons a week 10.00
Business College, rate on request.
Board and room, six weeks 43.50
Irregular meals, each........................... .35
Chemistry, Laboratory fee 10.00
Physics, Laboratory fee 6.00
Breakage fee, balance returnable 3.00

All fees are due at the time of enrollment, and will be collected at the main office of the University.

VALUE OF SUMMER CREDITS

In order that the summer work may be equal to that of any other term and the credits of the same value, the teachers are required by a set schedule to give as many hours of recitation to a branch of study in the summer terms as in other terms. Accordingly, credits received for summer work will count at full value for any college degrees or State teachers' certificates. Official time schedules of recitations will be bulletined in the main building some time before the summer term opens.

A. CAMPUS SCENE

T. C. U. campus is being constantly beautified with shrubbery, and recently the city arranged for a brilliant lighting system.

COURSES OF INSTRUCTION

The following courses are to be offered in the Summer School. The University may substitute or add another branch if the number of pupils should be sufficient to justify the work in any study.

CHEMISTRY AND PHYSICS
Professor John Davis.

The courses in science here offered are adapted, not only to the general student, but to those who are taking pre-medical studies. Especial emphasis this year for pre-medical students is laid upon the subject of physics.

The attention of the prospective medical students is particularly invited to the courses of study offered by this University. Pre-medical work is fully outlined in the University catalogue and carefully followed throughout the year. Also for some years this University has favored medical students with a combined course of literary and medical studies leading in six years to the two degrees A. B. and M. D.. This course is also fully set forth in the annual catalogue, and the Summer School in science is a part of this course.

11. **General Inorganic Chemistry**, nine credits to Freshmen and Sophomores, seven credits to Juniors and Seniors. Lectures, recitations and laboratory work. This course does not necessarily pre-suppose high school chemistry.

17. **General College Physics**, nine credits. Lectures, recitations and laboratory work. This course pre-supposes high school physics.

EDUCATION
Professors Wilson and McDiarmid.

A first grade State certificate, valid for four years, to teach in any public school in Texas is obtainable by completing forty-five college credits including nine credits in education. Accordingly the summer course in this department covers its work for the State certificate.

11. **Educational Psychology**, three credits. The aim is to apply psychological theory to educational practices. Special emphasis will be placed upon recent experimental work in the psychology of instruction. An introductory course.

21. **History of Education**, three credits. Lectures, assigned readings and discussions, intended to show the relation between social, religious and intellectual changes and the conception of the aim, method, curriculum, and organization of educational procedure in various periods of corresponding conditions of society.

29. **Educational Hygiene**, three credits. A survey of hygienic conditions and needs in public schools of every grade.

32. Play and Playgrounds, three credits. The psychology of recreation and the conditions that best contribute to the true interest of play.

` 34. Modern Elementary Education, three credits. A study of the social conditions, the educational theory, and the school practice of the reform movements in elementary education, including such reformers as Rousseau, Pestalozzi, Herbert, Froebel, and such modern movements as those represented by Francis Parker, Dewey, and Montessori.

39. Principles of Education, three credits.

Four of the above courses, in all twelve credits, will be offered, and they will be selected according to demand. Any student may take as many as nine credits.

ENGLISH
Professor Bryson.

11. Rhetoric and Composition, three credits. The work of the spring term will be offered.

39. The Modern Drama, three credits. The course will include the study of Ibsen and later dramatists, and the reading of representative modern plays.

42. Contemporary Poetry, three credits.

ENGLISH BIBLE
Professor Lockhart.

31. Messianic prophecy, six credits. A survey of Old Testament prophets, and the bearing of their work on Messianic announcements. An exegetical study of all the leading passages of the Old Testament that are justly regarded as Messianic.

HISTORY
Professor Lockhart.

35. History of Ancient Babylonia, three credits. The material for this course is drawn chiefly from the monuments excavated from the ruins of ancient Babylonian cities.

36. History of Ancient Assyria, three credits. Frequent reference will be made to the inscriptions of Assyrian kings and the relations of the Assyrians to the Hebrews of their day.

37. History of Ancient Egypt, three credits. The course will be supplemented by a consideration of the monumental sources of the history as developed by recent research.

MATHEMATICS
Professor Alexander.

11. Solid Geometry, three credits.
12. Plane Trigonometry, three credits.
13. College Alegbra, three credits.
14. Surveying, three credits. This course will include all the ordinary problems of the practical land surveyor; also differential and profile leveling.

23. Astronomy, three credits. A brief course in descriptive astronomy, requiring a knowledge of mathematics through solid geometry.

Four of the five courses listed above will be offered according to the demand.

MODERN LANGUAGES

FRENCH

Professor Richards.

A. **First Year French,** nine credits.

Studies of Fontaine's French Grammar; reading of French plays. Conversation in French will form an essential part of the course.

11-12. **Second Year French,** nine credits.

Conversation in French, study of grammar and composition; reading of interesting French novels and plays of Victor Hugo, Dumas, and Daudet.

SPANISH

A. **First Year Spanish,** nine credits.

Study of Hill & Ford's Spanish Grammar; conversation in Spanish, and reading of easy Spanish text.

Note: Other courses in French and Spanish will be offered if demand justifies it.

PHILOSOPHY

Professor McDiarmid.

Two of the three following courses will be offered, selected according to demand.

21. **Elementary Psychology,** three credits.
22. **Elementary Logic,** three credits.
23. **Elementary Ethics,** three credits.

POLITICAL SCIENCE
Professor E. R. Cockrell.

Two courses, three credits each, will be offered by the department this summer.

36. **International Law,** with special reference to our new international relationships. This course gives credits in both law and regular college work.

31. **New Problems** of Labor and Capital. This is a college course dealing with many present and vital issues.

SUMMER SCHOOL OF LAW

SUMMER FACULTY

E. R. COCKRELL, A. M., LL. M., Dean.
R. E. ROUER, LL. B., Attorney and Professor.
P. E. STEARNS, A. B., LL. B., Attorney and Professor.

The faculty of the Law School will organize classes for all who desire to pursue legal studies during the summer school. Our recently passed laws, raising requirements for those who desire to take examinations for admittance to the bar, enlarge our opportunity in this field. Those who desire to prepare for examination for the bar, as well as those who desire to get their class standing "regular," and those who just desire to "save time" can each be assisted by the Summer Law School.

A law just passed gives the T. C. U. College of Law the right to grant a license to practice law at the same time it grants its diploma. The wise student will obtain both a license and a diploma from a college of law recognized by our Supreme Court.

SUMMER SCHOOL OF MUSIC

PIANO
Professor Doering.

Mr. Carl Rupp Doering graduated at the Sternberg School of Music at Philadelphia and at the Leipzig Royal Conservatory of Music at Leipzig, Germany.

He is a pupil of Constantin von Sternberg and Robert Teichmuller.

The summer course of six weeks will be directed toward the needs and demands of music teachers and will include the subjects of Piano Technic and Aesthetics, Interpretation and Musical Form in their relations to piano playing.

Fees: Two half-hour periods per week; $21 for the term of six weeks. One period per week; $13 for the term.

Mrs. Doering.

Mrs. Doering will offer a course in Modern Piano servatory of Music of Leipzig, Germany, and was an assistant of Robert Teichmuller, director of the Leipzig Conservatory.

Mrs. Doering will offer a course in Modern Piano Technic, based upon the latest developments of the Weight and Relaxation Method of playing.

This method was reduced to a science by Teichmuller from the wonderful art of Rubinstein and Liszt, and consists (1) in eliminating unnecessary muscular contractions, saving fatigue and adding ease and velocity; (2) in giving proper weight to body, arm, hand, finger, so as to escape a cramped and stiffened movement and to produce a full, rich tone. Mrs. Doering will offer this very valuable method for professional students and teachers of music. She will be glad to give in advance to persons interested further information concerning the Weight and Relaxation Method.

Fees: Two half-hour periods per week, $21 for six weeks. One period per week, $13 for six weeks.

VOICE
Mrs. Cahoon.

Helen Fouts Cahoon is a singer who has received her musical training in America, under such well known artists as the late Max Heinrich, Max Bendix, and Walter S. Young, all of New York City, and recently under Charles W. Clark, of Chicago.

As director of the College of Music of Texas Christian University and as head of the Voice Department, Mrs. Cahoon has for several years had pupils from all of the United States whose beautiful singing is an evidence of her ability as a most successful teacher.

In reference to some recent work with him, Mr. Charles W. Clark wrote the following:

"My Dear Mrs. Cahoon:'

"It has been a great pleasure and privilege to work with you this summer, and I hope I have been able to give you inspiration and some points worth while.   -

"It was always such a joy to hear you sing that I may have passed over some minor points of no consequence, for it was difficult to find anything to criticize.

"Wishing you the greatest success," etc.

"CHAS. W. CLARK."

$22.50 for six weeks, for two lessons, $13.00 for one lesson, per week.

VIOLIN
Frederick M. Cahoon.

Mr. Cahoon has for several years been head violinist and director of the band and orchestra in T. C. U., and is known in the city and widely in the State as a most accomplished musician and teacher. He will offer work in violin and other instruments during the Summer School. Two lessons a week $18.00.

STUDIES WITH PROFESSOR ZIEGLER

Professor Samuel P. Ziegler studied Cello under D. Rendrick Ezerman, of Amsterdam, Holland, now head of Philadelphia Musical Academy, who was a pupil of the point and fugue under Richard Zickwer, President of Philadelphia Musical Academy, who was a pupil of the great Richter; for two years member of Faculty of Philadelphia Musical Academy.

CELLO

1. Fundamental exercises, scales, etc.

2. Etudes, duets, and easy pieces.

3. Advanced etudes, solos, and concert pieces.

Two lessons a week, twelve lessons, $18.00.

HARMONY

The study of scales, intervals, triads, seventh chords, and their inversions.

Easy modulations, suspensions, and Harmonization of melodies.

Two lessons a week, tuition fee, class $6.00, private $10.00.

COUNTERPOINT

Simple counterpoint in two, three, and four parts.

Same terms as Harmony.

HISTORY OF MUSIC

Beginning of Opera, Oratorio and Instrumental Music; Composers of Classic and Romantic Schools; Modern Music and Composers.

Terms same as Harmony.

PUBLIC SCHOOL MUSIC
Professor Ziegler.

The design of these courses is to prepare men and women to teach music in the public and high schools.

Teachers and Supervisors of music in public schools must be qualified to teach Harmony, History of Music, Sight Singing, and Musical Appreciation. They will need also a well rounded education and a love for the work. Some knowledge of string and wind instruments used in the orchestra is recommended. Hence the following courses are offered:

1. **Ear Training.**

Pitch, Rhythm and Notation which represents them

Chord recognition, simple modulation, and transposition. One hour a week. Tuition $6.00.

2. **Sight Singing.** Singing in common keys, beginning with simplest problems in pitch and rhythm; two, three, and four part singing. One hour a week, tuition fee $6.00.

3. **Public School Music.** Methods and material for teaching in primary and grammar grades.

High School methods. Outlines of teaching Harmony, Musical History and Musical Appreciation.

Musical Activities, including preparation of programs, etc.

One hour a week, tuition fee $6.00.

THE ART STUDIO

SUMMER SESSION OF THE ART DEPARTMENT

Mrs. Cockrell, Principal.

The Art Department will hold its usual summer session of six weeks. A term's work can be done in this length of time, as a lesson is given every morning, six days in the week, from eight until twelve o'clock.

This summer term of the Art Department has come to be one of the most successful of the whole year. All students remaining for it are seriously intent upon accomplishing as much as possible. There are very few diverting activities at this time of the year, and because of fewer pupils the instructor can give much personal attention to each one.

The art rooms are well situated for summer work, being in the main building, where they are cool and well ventilated, and all surroundings are conductive to good work.

Mrs. Cockrell will have charge of the summer work with what assistance is necessary according to the size of the class. The following branches will be taught:

Charcoal Drawing.

Oil, Water-color and Pastel Painting.

Tapestry.

China Painting.

Art Supervisor's Course.

Reconstruction Course.

Tuition for the entire term of six weeks is $20.00. Less time may be taken at a proportionate division of price.

SCHOOL OF ORATORY

Miss Leila Long Powell, Principal.

Three teachers of very high standing are employed through the regular session and they have large patronage in the University. They give instruction according to the celebrated Cummock method. Their work includes the development of the emotional nature which with vividness of imagination is the secret of eloquence. They lay stress on the thorough study of English, rhetoric and literature, on the control of the breath, distinct articulation, development of the emotional nature. Throughout the course the student is taught to strive for earnestness, naturalness, sincerity and simplicity. Stress is laid on the thorough study of English, rhetoric and literature, on the control of the breath, distinct articulation, the natural and orotund voices, force, pitch, rate, quality, emphasis and gesture.

Students are taught how throat difficulties occasioned by wrong use of vocal organs, may be avoided, how a pure and musical quality may be acquired and how awkwardness and mannerisms may be overcome.

Practical training is abundant in recitals, plays, dramas, declamatory contests, and oratorical and debating contests to which the University lends liberal encouragement. Various prizes from $5 to $20 are offered during the year for first and second places in these contests.

This department also has charge of the physical culture of the young women of the University. This work includes gymnastics, floor work, rhythm, games, swimming, pantomine and pageantry.

A regular course in oratory leading to graduation, embracing certain branches in the College of Arts and Sciences, has been defined. Such a graduation may be attained while the student is pursuing the regular work for an A. B. degree.

Work in the School of Oratory will be offered during the summer school by Miss Crisp, a post graduate of the School of Oratory. Fee, six weeks $10.00.

SUMMER SCHOOL OF HOME ECONOMICS

Purpose of the School

The primary object of this school is to develop young women in all womanly ways and graces and prepare them to become worthy makers and preservers of the home. The courses of study are prepared to secure for the student a thorough understanding of home-making.

The purpose is to supply a scientific study of foods, clothing, shelter, and the care of the sick, serving the ends of economy, art, health, and convenience.

Equipment

Large rooms in the Administration Building of the University have been well furnished with individual gas stoves and every modern article that may contribute to the latest and most practical methods of cooking. Likewise ample equipment is at hand for sewing and dressmaking. A strictly modern dining room has been fitted out for this Department. The University has regular department for Chemistry, General Economics, Bacteriology and Painting, all of which are available for students of this school.

DOMESTIC SCIENCE
Miss Gladys Turner, Principal.

Cooking and Serving 12, three credits, if Chemistry precede.

1. A study of the production, manufacture, and composition of typical foods, their classification according to the food principles and the study of the relation to the needs of the body.

2. A study of the cookery processes and their application to the cooking of typical foods.

3. A study of the principles involved in the cleaning and caring for the various sorts of utensils and materials found in the kitchen.

Tuition fee, $22.00.

Meal Serving 22, three credits, if Cooking 12 and Chemistry precede. Special stress on cost, conservation and proper balancing of menus to meet body requirements and to appeal to the esthetic sense.

DOMESTIC ART

Sewing 12, three credits.

This course is arranged for those wishing to begin sewing in the elementary form. Learning the stitches, both plain and decorative, and the making of simple garments is given special stress. Patterns used will be drafted by the students. Tuition $8.00.

Sewing 22, three credits, if sewing 12 and Textiles 22 precede. Pre-requisite, Sewing 12 or its equivalent. Blouses and dresses are made with a certain amount allowed for the expenditure of each. Tuition fee $8.00.

Textiles 22.

Pre-requisite, Chemistry 11 or 14. Study of the different fibers, their growth, manufacture, etc. Also the weaving and spinning processes. Testing of wool, cotton, and silk for adulterations and impurities. Tuition $3.

T. C. U. COLLEGE OF BUSINESS SUMMER SCHOOL

The College of Business will offer full courses in book-keeping, shorthand, typewriting and penmanship together with their accompanying branches during the summer. As these courses are individual courses, the student may enter any time and give as much or as little time as he may desire to each course. Either of the courses may be taken in connection with University or Academy work.

Take these helpful business training courses during the summer and be ready to accept a position in the fall should you decide to not re-enter the University. You can get the training in T. C. U. College of Business that will enable you to step right into a $1,000 or $1,200 place. We have had more calls for competent bookkeepers and stenographers this year than we could supply.

Rates for the different courses given upon request. Write or see us about this immediately.

T. C. U. COLLEGE OF BUSINESS,

J. A. Dacus, Superintendent.

THE ACADEMY

The Academy connected with Texas Christian University offers the usual high school course of study, however, with many better facilities than most high schools possess as respects library and laboratories. The rate of tuition per unit course undertaken will be $16. The following courses are provisionally announced:

LATIN
Mr. Riley Aiken.

Caesar and Prose Composition, one unit.

MATHEMATICS

Second Year Algebra, one unit.
Plane Geometry, one unit.

PHYSICS
Mr. O. B. Douglass.

Elementary Physics, with laboratory experiments, one unit.

SPANISH
Mr. Riley Aiken.

One unit, at least, in Spanish will be offered, subject to demand.

ENGLISH
Teacher to be selected

American Literature with composition and rhetoric, one unit.
English Literature with advanced composition, one unit.

HISTORY
Teacher to be selected

Medieval and Modern History, one unit.
History of England, one unit.

Note: The above courses are proposed with the reservation that in case the demand should seem insufficient, any course may be omitted and the student will be offered choice of other studies.

THE COLLEGE BRED MAN IN BUSINESS AND IN POLITICS

DR. CHARLES THWING made a study of fifteen thousand one hundred forty-two eminent men mentioned in Appleton's Encyclopedia of American Biography to find the facts especially with regard to the relation between college training and success in political life and in amassing wealth. Of the one hundred wealthiest men in the United States he found that in proportion to the total number in America possessing a college education there were 277 times as many college-bred men who had amassed great wealth as there were of noncollege-bred men. In proportion to their numbers in the population, the college men have become Members of the National House of Represntativs 352 times as often as the noncollege-bred men; Members of the Senate 350 times as often; President 1,392 times as often; Justices of the Supreme Court 2,027 times as often. Of the more than 10,000 prominent and successful men in all lines mentioned who were still living, 58 per cent were college graduates, and 75 per cent had had some college training. On the whole, the college bred man had attained enough eminence to be mentioned in such a cyclopedia 870 times as often in proportion to his number as the noncollege-bred man.

IN THE WAR that will follow after the war the school, the laboratory, and the workshop are to be the battlefields. The weapons which science places in the hands of those who engage in great rivalries of commerce leave those who are without them as badly off as were the Dervishes of Ondurman against the maxims of Lord Kitchener.

THE EDUCATED MIND IS the greatest producing agency in the world, without which fertile soil, timbered land, and mineral deposits are so much useless material. The state or the church that fails to educate dooms its children to industrial and intellectual servitude by those from that state or church that educates.